GOODBYE,
INSECURITIES,
AND
HELLO
GORGEOUS

GOODBYE, INSECURITIES, AND HELLO GORGEOUS

By Dr. Diana Lowe

ISBN: 978-1-961650-26-8 (Paperback)
ISBN: 978-1-961650-27-5 (e-book)

Printed in the United States of America.
Published in the United States by GeeMorgan Publishing
First printing edition 2024.
All inquiries about this book can be sent to the author at evangdlow@gmail.com or DianaLowe@geemorganpublishing.com

GeeMorgan Publishing
19046 Bruce B Downs Blvd #1016,
Tampa, FL 33647
www.geemorganpublishing.com

DEDICATION

This book is wholeheartedly dedicated first to the Holy Spirit, my unwavering guide and teacher through life's ups and downs.

To all the women battling with feelings of low self-esteem and insecurity, this book is for you. Your journey, struggles, and resilience have not gone unnoticed.

"If God is for us, who can be against us?" Remember, we are blessed in every step we take, from the moment we step out to the moment we return home.

Thank you for picking up this book. It is my deepest wish that as you walk this path of self-discovery with me, you will find yourself at the threshold of a bright and hopeful new beginning.

May the blessings of the Lord be upon you,

DL

ACKNOWLEDGEMENTS

I cannot fully express my gratitude to GeeMorgan Publishing for their invaluable expertise and dedication to making this book a reality.

I am grateful to Dr. Martha M. Hall, my spiritual guide and mentor. Your unwavering support and confidence have been my beacon. Thank you for being an indispensable confidant; you are always there when I need guidance.

To my friends Lynette Burroughs, Linda Blount, Carolyn Sellers, Maune Munford—who always believed in me—and Pastors Timothy and Claudette Williams, your encouragement has been a source of strength and motivation.

My family has been my cornerstone. To my sisters, Lisa and Brenda Neloms, and to my children, Darryl, Corinthus, Salynthia, Terrell, and T.J., your unwavering support and love have sustained me throughout this journey.

To all of you, my heartfelt love,
DL

TABLE OF CONTENTS

INTRODUCTION

Ephesians 2:10 tells us, *"We are God's masterpiece."* He has created us anew in Christ Jesus, enabling us to accomplish the good things He planned for us long ago. Often, we find ourselves struggling to discover significance in the ordinary aspects of life: in our moments of peace, within the confines of our homes, amidst the daily grind of our jobs, and in the essence of life itself—even deep within ourselves.

Caught in the grip of insecurity, with our spirits dampened by low self-esteem, existence can feel like a mere battle for survival. We find ourselves in a painful struggle, seeking to understand God's will in our immediate reality. This battle often breeds feelings of frustration, guilt, and dismay, obscuring the light of hope and guidance.

Consider the story of a young woman facing a harsh winter without adequate means to buy a new coat. Financial constraints made shopping at a department store an impossible dream, leaving her Heart heavy. Desperate, she entered a Goodwill store, silently praying that no one would witness her entry. The weather was cold outside, and she needed to purchase a coat to wear. Once inside, she purchased a coat and hurried home. In the solitude of her space, she discovered the coat's hidden treasures—two long zip pockets concealing valuable jewelry. This unexpected find served as a poignant reminder.

Our self-perceptions often fail to reflect the grandeur with which God views us. Like hidden treasures in a worn coat, our true worth awaits discovery. When we truly begin to feel the zest for life and the abundance of life that Jesus promised us, we will no longer feel trapped inside the walls of insecurity, low self-esteem, shyness, and fear.

This book aims to uplift you with scriptures that radiate comfort and positivity, nurturing your Heart and soul. You will explore how life's seemingly insurmountable challenges can lead to profound revelations and fresh beginnings when we place our trust in Jesus. Remember, you are remarkable; old things have passed away, and all things have become new. Embrace the journey ahead with love, joy, peace, and happiness as you pursue your renewed purpose.

CHAPTER ONE

POEM

Look At Me
Take a look at me
What do you see?
No, I am not sitting
Under a tree

Take a look at me
What do you see?
A changed person with
A lot of possibilities.

I am kind, I am pleasant
I am peace, oh can't you see.
Long life is in my right-hand
And riches and honor are in
My left hand.

Take a look at me
What do you see?
I am a tree of life to those
Who Embrace me.

AIM HIGH (LOW SELF-ESTEEM)

"Believe in yourself, know your worth, and don't let self-doubt hold you back. With determination, self-compassion, and a positive mindset, you can build unshakable self-confidence and conquer any challenge that comes your way."

"It is not what you are that is holding you back. It's what you think you are not."

"Attitude is a little thing that makes a big difference, it takes courage to grow up and become who you are."

"Find out who you are and be that person, Find that truth, be that truth, and live that truth to the fullest, and focus on the positive because that is the truth."

I f you dream of achieving big things, the first step is simple yet profound: ask Jesus for guidance and aim high. Jesus is always talking to us, but too often, we're too wrapped up in our plans and worries to listen. Have you ever thought about how often we've rushed ahead with our ideas only to watch everything fall apart? By placing Jesus at the forefront of our decisions and asking Him for directions on where to go or what to do, we open ourselves up to limitless possibilities.

Let us look into what it means to "AIM" Essentially, it is about setting your focus on a specific goal. Considering the word "HIGH" as well means at or to a high place, a high altitude, a high level, or a high degree. When considering this phrase "AIM HIGH," we say it does not matter what others think of us. The most important thing is how you see yourself—as a winner. Feeling fed up with starting over again and again? Here is a piece of advice:

- Do not give up.
- Keep pushing forward.
- Remember, winners never quit, and quitters never win.

Keep your eyes on the prize, and don't stop chasing it until you've reached that top level or achieved that ultimate goal.
With this determined mindset and Jesus as your guide, you can go anywhere.

Sometimes, when we're caught in the suffocating embrace of low self-esteem, life can feel like a relentless struggle. It is as if we are trapped within the confining walls of our doubts, losing faith in ourselves and in the goodwill of others. The wisdom found in Proverbs 3:5- 6 offers a beacon of hope: (5) *"Trust in the Lord with all your heart and lean not on your understanding;(6) in all your ways acknowledge him, and he will make your paths straight."* This passage gently reminds us to place our trust beyond our immediate perceptions and to find strength in faith.

Consider the story of a teenage girl deeply wounded by sexual assault. Her journey was marked by profound suffering, anger, and demeaning abuse. Daily, she was bombarded with cruel words, being told she was unworthy of love or affection because of her appearance and intelligence. These were not isolated incidents; she endured them repeatedly, isolated without a confidante. To add to her torment, her mother's verbal lashings were a daily ordeal, leaving her without a sanctuary. As days merged into weeks, she noticed the hollowness in the gestures of those around her, their feigned affection only deepening her sense of isolation.

She reached a point of despair, questioning the very value of her existence, feeling overwhelmed by her desire to escape her pain. Yet, even as she contemplated these dark thoughts, a part of her clung to hope, seeking reasons to endure. "Why does no one love me? Is it because of my weight, my looks, or am I truly as insignificant as they say?" Amidst her tears, in her moment of vulnerability, a soft, comforting voice reached out to her, saying, *"Before I formed you in the womb, I knew you, and before you were born, I set you apart"* (Jeremiah 1:5). This message, imbued with love and recognition, offered her a glimpse of her inherent value, reminding her that she was cherished and seen long before her struggles began.

You are my masterpiece, and I have plans for you. Jeremiah 29:11-14 *"For I know the thoughts that I think toward you, said the Lord, thoughts of peace and not of evil, to give you an expected end. Then shall you call upon me, and you shall go and pray to me, and I will hearken to you. And ye shall seek me and find me when ye shall search for me with all your heart. And I will be found of you, said the Lord."*

When you manage to put aside your pain, your disappointments, and the times you have been knocked down by others and get back up, that is when you truly shine. It is about letting go of the person you think you should be and embracing the person you are. Remember, even if no one else sees your worth, you should see it in yourself because you are a precious gem filled with undiscovered treasures.

Just like after every storm, the skies clear up, and nature revitalizes - the air freshens, birds sing, and flowers bloom, more vibrant than ever. John 1:16 reminds us, *"Out of his fullness we have all received grace in place of grace already given."*

We have all faced moments that pushed us to our limits and made us want to escape our pain and give up. But taking the easy way out solves nothing; it leaves us feeling empty. Overcoming these challenges is what shapes us.

Colossians 1:16,17 says, *"For in him all things were created: things in heaven and on earth, visible and invisible, whether thrones or powers or rulers or authorities; all things have been created through him and for him. He is before all things, and in him all things hold together."*

Remember, no matter what others say, how things might seem, or how you are treated, God holds everything in His hands. Always keep faith in your Heart and know that God's love means there is always hope for a brighter tomorrow. Psalm 46:1 says, *"God is our refuge and strength, an ever-present help in trouble."* This verse powerfully reminds us that no matter what challenges or difficulties we face in life, God is always there to offer us shelter and support. He is our steadfast protector and source of strength, especially in times when we feel most vulnerable. It is comforting to know that we are never alone in our struggles; we always have a sanctuary where we can find peace and resilience.

Philippians 4:13 states, *"I can do everything through Christ who strengthens me."* This verse is incredibly uplifting, emphasizing the boundless potential we have when we place our trust in Christ. It speaks to the Idea that, with faith, we are not limited by our weaknesses or the obstacles in our path. Instead, we are empowered to overcome any challenge and achieve our goals. It reassures us that our capabilities are not just our own but are amplified by the strength we receive from our faith in Christ.

Do you ever ponder the idea that there is always hope for tomorrow? Is that something you truly believe in? Can you gather the pieces of your life and step forward? Do you still find yourself grappling with insecurities? Starting afresh after enduring loss, adversity, and wrestling with insecurities is no easy feat. The emotional toll lingers, and it might seem like there is no light at the end of the tunnel. Insecurity has a way of haunting your nights with dreadful nightmares. It traps you indoors, convinced that the moment you step outside, you are under scrutiny or gossip. It is a suffocating feeling that confines you. But remember, it is not who you are that holds you back; it is the doubts about who you think you are not. Sometimes, to gain a better perspective on life's challenges, you need to navigate around them or climb a little higher.

The most breathtaking views come after the most strenuous climbs because you have triumphed over your weaknesses without surrendering, reaching your objectives. When you finally conquer that mountain and stand at its summit, you can breathe in the crisp air. You witness the sun's warmth and the stars twinkling above. It is at this moment that you begin to savor the love, joy, and happiness that reside within you.

Psalm 34:8 reminds us, *"O taste and see that the Lord is good; blessed is the man that trusted in him."* Happiness is found in a man's possession. His appreciation for beauty reflects his taste. Crafting his insecurities becomes his art. He expresses the emotions he has encountered. Insecurities can render you unproductive, consumed by fear of rejection, leading to misery and a lack of self-confidence, which you neither want nor need and can live without. Hold your head high and stand tall. Remember, how we perceive ourselves is not how God sees us. You are God's masterpiece, a precious jewel, highly esteemed, no longer confined within the walls of low self-esteem.

Goodbye Low Self-Esteem and Hello Gorgeous!

Chapter Review

1. **Seek Guidance and Set High Goals:** The importance of looking beyond oneself for direction and aiming for lofty aspirations is emphasized. By asking for Jesus' guidance and aiming high, one acknowledges the value of divine direction in achieving significant life goals.

2. **Perseverance in the Face of Adversity:** The narrative underscores the necessity of persistence and resilience. It highlights that overcoming challenges and not giving up on pursuing one's dreams is crucial for success.

3. **The Power of Faith and Trust:** Trusting in divine power and not leaning on one's understanding is presented as a pathway to overcoming obstacles and finding strength in moments of doubt and self-esteem issues.

4. **Recognition of Self-Worth:** The content highlights the importance of self-recognition and

valuing oneself beyond external validation. Understanding that one is a masterpiece with inherent value and purpose is crucial for combating low self-esteem.

5. **Empowerment through Faith:** The message reinforces that individuals are empowered to overcome any challenge and achieve their goals with faith. It stresses the belief that one's abilities are amplified through faith, enabling the transformation from self-doubt to confidence and achievement.

CHAPTER TWO

POEM

Let's look at Heart, Plans, Succeed,
The Heart is your center of Idea
The Plans which are more than one
Are your emotions and your thoughts.
Success is your motivation,
Courage, and action;
Make it happen, and just do it.

Live out your imagination and not your history.
Let the creation of the mind take place
The shyness disappears, and the boldness comes fore.
Don't give up on your dreams, if you do
Your dreams will give up on you
Remember, you have to dream before
Your dreams can come true.

Nothing in the world can take the place
of being persistence
when you reach an obstacle,
Turn it into an opportunity because
you have the choice to be a
LOSER or a WINNER
KEEP PRESSING

FROM DREAMING TO REALITY (SHYNESS)

"Success is a journey, not a destination. Do not be afraid to give up the good to pursue the great."

Albert Einstein said, "Imagination is more important than knowledge."

Psalm 20:4 *"May he give you the heart's desire and make all your plans succeed."* In biblical terms, the Heart is depicted as the core of our spiritual existence. From this central wellspring, our emotions emerge, our thoughts take shape, our motivations grow, our bravery is kindled, and our actions are born actions that nourish the very essence of life itself.

Consider the term "Dream": a fascinating series of thoughts, images, and emotions that dance through our minds as we sleep. Now, juxtapose that with "Reality": "The quality or state of being real". Dreams visit us all, occasionally brushing our consciousness with their ethereal presence. But there comes a moment, a sacred whisper in time, when God plants a dream so vivid, so stirring within you, that it ignites a fervent zeal. In these divine instances, we must pause, listen intently, and decode the message being conveyed through our dreams. Many of us, at one point or another, stand at the crossroads where our shyness overshadows our dreams and opportunities for success.

Shyness, with its cold, clammy hands, can deter us from our path, making us hesitant and recoiling at the thought of stepping into the spotlight or committing to actions that might expose us to the gaze of many. I, too, have stood behind the imposing wall of insecurity, shackled by my shyness. I've felt the weight of hesitation, the reluctance to put myself out there, especially in scenarios that demanded I stand before a crowd. If this resonates with you, let me share a piece of wisdom hard-earned from my journey. It is in acknowledging our vulnerabilities that we find our strength. Shyness is not a prison; it is a challenge to overcome, a layer to peel back on the way to uncovering the full magnitude of our potential. When God entrusts you with a dream, it is not by accident. It is a call to action—a signal that it is time to move, shake off the chains of fear, and step into the light of your destiny. So, to you who might be wrestling with shyness, feeling

its grip tighten around your dreams, I say: look beyond the wall.

Your dreams are not just fleeting shadows of the night; they are beacons guiding you towards your purpose. Embrace them with open arms, step forward with courage, and let the world see the brilliance of your light. Remember, in the universes' grand design, you are here for a reason. Your dreams, your voice, your story—it all matters. Take the stage that life has set for you and let the beauty of your dreams unfold into reality.

I remember my college days, studying Early Childhood Education. One class, Personal Psychology for Life and Work particularly stood out. Our instructor assigned each of us a topic to discuss, using index cards as our cue cards, limiting us to ten words or less. While sitting at your desk was comfortable, standing in front of the class was terrifying. When it was my turn to present my topic, I was overwhelmed with nerves and fear. My legs shook like maracas, and my knees knocked as though to a drumbeat. I knew I had to push through, or I would fail the class. My fear stemmed from my intense shyness about speaking in front of everyone. However, as I began to speak, I realized it wasn't as bad as I had feared. With each class presentation, my shyness diminished. Ultimately, I passed the class with a B average. Now, I stand before people as a pastor, preaching God's word and singing.

2 Timothy 1:7 tells us, "For God did not give us a spirit of timidity, but a spirit of power, love, and self-discipline." Reflecting on my past, I understand now that my fears and anxieties were self-imposed, born from the mistaken belief that standing before others would automatically rob me of confidence. Over the months and years, God introduced me to R.A.W.

Righteous Anointed Women (R.A.W)

What is **R.A.W.**? It is a ministry dedicated to healing, deliverance, and counselling, focusing particularly on helping women who have suffered abuse and neglect and struggle with low self-esteem reclaim their dignity and character by addressing their physical, emotional, financial, and spiritual well-being. Founded in 2008, the ministry did not fully come to life until 2009. Through this ministry, many individuals have found their way back, rejuvenated through God's complete guidance. You might wonder how this relates to dreams and reality. Let me explain - Dreams are the creative visions of our thoughts and images, the cradle of all human creativity that gestates and flourishes in our imagination.

Genesis 1:1 states, *"In the beginning, God created the heavens and the earth."* Before anything came into being, it existed as a thought in God's mind. He had a vision for something that did not yet exist. By speaking it into existence, God demonstrated He is the ultimate creator, dreamer, author, and artist. It all sprang from His imagination; from the vision He conceived in His mind. God envisioned a dream and then brought it to life with His words. We, too, share this divine capacity to dream about things that haven't happened yet and to witness those dreams unfold into reality. We must overcome shyness, timidity, and lack of confidence to progress with our dreams. To realize these dreams or goals, one needs self-motivation, driven by ambition or willpower, and physical vitality.

Hebrews 11:1 states, *"Now faith is the substance of things hoped for, the evidence of things not seen"*.

Consider a young man who, during his school years, was shy and reluctant to stand in front of his class despite having an A average. He preferred to remain in the background. He dreamt of owning a large house and a convertible car. After graduating high school, he joined the military, replacing his shyness with boldness. Today, he runs his own business and has achieved his dreams of a house and a convertible car.

A dream inspired by God is fueled by His will, passion, and abilities. My dreams were guided by God's will, seeded with passion, and nurtured with abundant abilities. You will find it impossible if you believe you cannot achieve something. But when you believe you can, you suddenly possess the means to do it, even if you did not initially have the capability. Transitioning from dreaming to reality requires a positive self-view and belief in oneself. This changes how one responds to situations, leading to more favorable outcomes. Remember, Psalm 20:4 says, *"May He give you the desire of your heart and make all your plans succeed."*

In the journey of bringing your dreams to life, challenges are inevitable. Your dreams are precious seeds waiting to blossom into reality, but the path ahead will not always be smooth. Despite the obstacles that may come your way, your commitment to setting goals acts as the bridge between your aspirations and their fulfillment. There will be moments when the road ahead feels daunting, and the temptation to give up looms large. However, it is during these trying times that your determination must shine brightest. Push yourself out of that slump, summon the strength to persevere, and continue the journey you have embarked upon.

One crucial lesson to remember is not to allow the opinions of others to dictate the pursuit of your dreams. Your dreams are uniquely yours, and only you hold the key to their realization. While others may offer their perspectives, the final decision rests with you. Stay focused on your path, undeterred by external voices, and takes each step forward with unwavering resolve. Every great dream begins with a dreamer—an individual who dares to envision a brighter future and is willing to chase after it relentlessly. Along the way, you may encounter naysayers who seek to belittle your ambitions. But remember, the length of the journey matters less than the steadfastness of your commitment. Hold fast to your dreams, regardless of the time it takes to achieve them. Within each of us lies a treasure trove of dreams, aspirations, and desires waiting to be unearthed. To bring these dreams to fruition, take the time to identify them, break them down into manageable goals, and craft a roadmap for success. By setting clear objectives and devising an actionable plan, you pave the way for your dreams to become a reality. So, dare to dream, pursue your passions with purpose, and watch as your aspirations take flight.

Ephesians 3:20 reassures us, *"Now unto him that is able to do exceedingly abundantly above all that we ask or think, according to the power that worketh in us."* An incredible force of goodness is at work in your life, surpassing even your boldest dreams. Despite any reservations or shyness you may feel, believe that great things are on the horizon.

Shift your mindset away from thoughts of scarcity and embrace thoughts of prosperity and abundance. Know that the best is yet to come, awaiting your embrace. Your shyness may have served as a crutch, holding you back from stepping into your full potential. But as you

25

release this prop and recognize your own inner strength, you will be amazed at what you can achieve.

Stepping beyond the confines of your comfort zone opens your eyes to the beauty of the world around you. It is like seeing everything anew for the very first time. Now, as you courageously move forward, leaving behind anything that hinders your progress, including your shyness, trust that God has granted the desires of your heart and fulfilled your deepest dreams. Remain steadfast in your determination to progress, seeking guidance from wise believers and aligning yourself with God's will. Let gratitude fill your heart as you follow the path that God has laid before you.

Goodbye Fearfulness, and Hello Gorgeous!

Chapter Review

1. **The Power of Dreams in Guiding Our Lives:**
    The chapter emphasizes how dreams, those vivid
    thoughts, images, and emotions we experience, are
    not mere flights of fancy but divine nudges guiding
    us towards our purpose. It encourages us to listen
    and act on these dreams, seeing them as the
    creative visions that propel us from imagination to
    reality.

2. **Overcoming Shyness to Realize Our
    Dreams**: It speaks to the common challenge of
    shyness that can stifle our potential and hinder our
    progress towards our dreams. The narrative shares
    a personal journey of overcoming this barrier,
    highlighting the importance of confronting and
    moving beyond our fears to embrace the
    opportunities that await us.

3. **The Role of Faith and Self-Belief:** The chapter
    underscores the significance of faith and self-belief
    in the journey from dreaming to achieving. It

reminds us that believing in our capacity to succeed, spurred by faith, is fundamental in transforming our dreams into reality.

4. **The Importance of Taking Action:** The chapter advocates for the necessity of action through personal anecdotes and motivational quotes. It encourages starting small but insists on the importance of starting as the critical step towards turning dreams into achievements, emphasizing persistence and resilience in the face of obstacles.

5. **Divine Inspiration and Human Potential:** Lastly, the chapter explores the concept that we are all capable of divine-inspired creativity and dreams. It suggests that just as God created with a vision, we too can dream and create our futures, underlining the divine aspect of our creative endeavors and the boundless potential within us to achieve our dreams.

CHAPTER
THREE

POEM

Roots of Change
In life's vast garden, weeds may sprout,
Echoing fears, casting doubt.
Yet within us lies the power,
To root them out, hour by hour.

With resolve as sharp as a spade,
We excavate the shade,
Unearthing habits, old and grim,
To let the light of change within.

Step by step, and day by day,
We clear the old and make way for new ways.
For growth is not without its about,
In strength, we root the darkness out.

ROOTING IT OUT

"Grow in the root of all grace, which is in Faith."

"If you know where you are from, it's harder for people to stop you where you are going."

"It does not matter how slowly you go as long as you do not stop. It always seems impossible until you do it. Our greatest weakness lies in giving up."

Proverbs 14:30 "A heart at peace gives life to the body."

Jeremiah 32:27 states, *"I am the Lord, the God of all mankind. Is anything too hard for Me?"* The unequivocal answer is no. Within the bounds of God's will, including the creation and redemption, nothing is deemed impossible for Him. God embodies omnipotence, endowed with the capacity to execute any act according to His will. Yet, He remains incapable of actions that conflict with His divine essence, such as overlooking sin, engaging in absurdities, or performing self-contradictory acts. Unlike being at the mercy of His omnipotence, God maintains absolute sovereignty over His power. His deservingness of our obedience is rooted in His unwavering fidelity to His promises.

The term "Rooting" is described as completely eradicating something, akin to extracting it from its roots. Pride sits at the core of all sin, manifesting in our reluctance to acknowledge errors or to concede the need for assistance. For a doctor to effectively administer treatment to a patient, the primary objective is to ascertain the underlying cause of the symptoms. Once he discovers the cause of the problem, he begins addressing the root of the issue. Numerous types of roots must be eradicated, For example, nicotine, alcohol, gambling, drugs, dishonesty, fear, and compulsive behavior, to mention a few. Negative self-talk is the most challenging habit to overcome. It is an invisible adversary many of us are unaware of. If the root causes of our problems are not addressed, they will only grow more severe.

Hebrews 12:15 warns, *"Look carefully lest anyone fall short of the grace of God; lest any root of bitterness springing up causes trouble, and by this, many become defiled."* We must actively seek and eliminate the roots of sinful behavior. In the Gospels of Luke and John, we find two distinct stories: one about a rich man and another involving a multitude of disciples. Both illustrate the refusal to confront root issues in their lives.

In Luke 18:18-23, we encounter the Rich Ruler, a young, morally upright, law-abiding man. Despite his faithfulness to God's commandments, he had a significant issue that needed correction. His wealth was more important to him than his commitment to the Lord. When Jesus invited him to sell his possessions and follow Him, the young man chose to walk away, thereby missing his divine destiny. This individual was not interested in addressing his underlying issues; his wealth was too precious, and sacrificing everything was not a solution for him. Jesus desires for us to be happy, wealthy, and successful. However, wealth and success are only as beneficial or detrimental as how one chooses to use them.

1 Timothy 6:10 states, *"For the love of money is a root of all kinds of evil."* This powerful warning reminds us that when we elevate money to the status of an idol, we inadvertently align ourselves with evil. The rich young man's story illustrates this peril, as he values his wealth more than his relationship with Jesus. In John 6:60-66, we learn about the disciples who turned away from Jesus. These individuals, followers of Jesus at that time, were initially drawn by His profound teachings and the miracles He performed. Despite their enthusiasm, the reality of discipleship—as Jesus defined it—proved too challenging for many to accept. They preferred to learn and be amazed by miracles but found the truth of

Jesus's teachings hard to embrace, leading them to reject His words and revert to their previous lives.

The core issue in both scenarios is the refusal to confront and address the root causes of their spiritual dilemmas. Whether it is the love of money or the inability to accept challenging teachings, these root causes can derail one's Faith and commitment. Many people today mirror the rich young ruler or the deserting disciples, choosing earthly comforts over spiritual growth. However, it is essential to remember that it is never too late to confront and eradicate these detrimental roots from our lives. Habits, whether good or bad, form through repeated behavior until they become almost automatic. But they can become obstacles, affecting every aspect of life—from work and personal wellbeing to relationships and health. Overcoming a harmful habit requires a firm decision to quit and the discipline to stick to that decision. Making excuses for "just one more time" reinforces the old patterns. Letting go of these habits without exceptions is crucial for genuine change.

1 Samuel 17 recounts the story of a formidable challenger from the Philistine camp, Goliath, who

stood nine feet and nine inches tall. This giant posed a significant threat and was a deep-rooted issue for the Israelites. For forty days, he dared any Israelite to combat him, instilling fear throughout their camp. Then came David, a young shepherd, who accepted the challenge, recognizing it was time to remove Goliath from the Israelites' lives. Armed with only a slingshot, which he wielded with skill, and five smooth stones from a brook, David was prepared not just for Goliath but potentially his four sons, should they seek vengeance.

David's victory over Goliath, with God's guidance, symbolizes the triumph of Faith and courage over seemingly insurmountable challenges. This story illustrates that the "giants" in our lives—our habits, problems, and fears—can be overcome by trusting in the Lord and facing them with determination. David's approach to confronting Goliath teaches believers the power of Faith in the Lord Jesus, encouraging them to trust in God wholeheartedly and to recognize Him in all their ways. It is a testament to bravery, courage, and Faith, showing that those who confront their giants with a faithful heart can achieve victory.

Similarly, the story of Mrs. Bonnie, who began smoking at seventeen to fit in, mirrors the concept of following the crowd without recognizing the harm of her actions. Like the sheep following through the gate, she didn't see the health consequences of smoking a pack of cigarettes a day. Mrs. Bonnie's experience emphasizes the importance of making independent, healthy choices rather than succumbing to peer pressure or habits that lead to self-destruction. Over the years, Mrs. Bonnie developed a strong addiction to nicotine, smoking two packs of cigarettes daily for thirty-eight years. At fifty-five, she was rushed to the hospital due to a heart attack. The surgery required veins from her left leg to be used in creating new arteries for her heart, and she also lost one kidney. Her nicotine habit was the "giant" in her life, leading to a heart attack and the loss of a kidney. Today, she expresses deep gratitude for the second chance at life God has given her. Nicotine addiction is a destructive force that gradually overtakes you. The only way to overcome it is to eradicate it, starting from its roots.

The term "rooting out" means eliminating something by removing it at the roots. To break a habit, one must first acknowledge the habit and then feel motivated to change behavior. Sometimes, external support is necessary to break free from these habits. Joining support groups or watching educational films about the dangers of smoking can be effective first steps in addressing the issue. It is crucial to pay attention to all habit patterns before they become entrenched and actively work to change harmful ones. Delaying action often leads to excuses, minimizing the importance of change.

Understanding how a habit is formed initially can illuminate ways to modify or eliminate the environment that sustains it, aiding in the habit-breaking process. Tackle your habit-breaking journey one day at a time, renewing your commitment daily until you have addressed the issue at its root and completely removed it. To cultivate a stunning flower garden, remove all the weeds from their roots; otherwise, the weeds will overtake and suffocate the flowers.

To effectively address any root issue, you must:

- Define the problem.
- Collect data—what evidence do you have that the problem exists?
- Identify possible causal factors.
- Determine the root cause(s).
- Recommend and implement solutions.

The goal is to eliminate the roots, not to keep them completely. Therefore, you must dig deep to find and remove them. The type of roots does not matter; persistence is key. Let us begin and tackle those roots.

When you root out a person or a habit, you are essentially evicting them from their current place of residence; they are no longer welcome or permitted to remain. Similarly, when you root out a problem or an unpleasant circumstance, you are identifying its source and putting an end to it. Often, the root cause of a problem or situation is concealed from plain sight, and the longer it festers unchecked, the more detrimental it becomes.

The "root" of a plant, much like a flower, extends deep into the earth, anchoring itself firmly in the soil. To rid your garden of weeds, you must dig deep and extract them from the root. Simply cutting off the top won't suffice.

When confronted with challenges, habits, or issues in your life—be they corruption, illegal activity, or intangible struggles—they all require removal by rooting them out of your life. Habits, in particular, act as deep-seated roots. Whether it's smoking cigarettes while drinking or constantly lying to impress others, habits such as these must be eradicated from their very core. Whether tangible or intangible, addressing both the tangible and intangible aspects is crucial in uprooting these detrimental influences from your life.

Chapter Review

1. **Divine Omnipotence and Human Responsibility:** Jeremiah 32:27 underscores God's limitless power in the face of human challenges, reminding us that nothing is too hard for God within His will. This teaches us to rely on divine strength while recognizing our role in combating negative habits and behaviors.

2. **The Nature of Sin and the Need for Awareness:** The chapter highlights pride as the root of all sin, showing how it manifests in our reluctance to admit faults or seek help. This insight urges us to cultivate humility and self-awareness as critical steps towards personal growth and overcoming bad habits.

3. **The Importance of Addressing Root Causes:** Just as a doctor aims to treat the underlying cause of a symptom, we learn the importance of ascertaining and addressing the root causes of our spiritual and behavioral challenges. This approach

ensures lasting changes rather than temporary fixes.

4. **The Power of Faith in Overcoming Challenges:** The story of David and Goliath taught us that Faith and courage can help us conquer our "giants"—be they habits, fears, or problems. David's victory symbolizes the triumph over obstacles through trust in God and determination.

5. **The Role of Persistence and External Support in Breaking Habits:** The chapter discusses the necessity of acknowledging bad habits, feeling motivated to change, and sometimes seeking external support to overcome them. It emphasizes that breaking a habit is a process that requires persistence, time, and sometimes the help of others through support groups or educational resources.

CHAPTER FOUR

POEM

In the heart of the storm, I stand firm, unswayed,
With a fierce spirit, my resolve never frayed.
"Nothing but Greatness," I whisper to the night,
An overcomer, I am born to conquer, to fight.
Through valleys so deep, where shadows hold sway,
I march forth with courage, turning night into day.
No mountain too steep, no ocean too wide,
With every step forward, my hope is my guide.
In the mirror, the victor's reflection I see,
"Nothing but Greatness" — it's my destiny.
I am an overcomer; with each trial, I grow,
A beacon of strength, in my heart, I know.
So I'll rise and I'll soar beyond what I've known,
In the garden of greatness, my seeds have been sown.
For I am an overcomer, and this truth I hold dear,
With every challenge I face, I conquer my fear.

NOTHING BUT GREATNESS, I AM AN OVERCOMER

"You must be the change you wish to see in the world"

"Darkness cannot drive out darkness; only light can do that."

"People often say that motivation doesn't last, and neither does bathing, which is why we recommend it daily."

"Stay positive, and you will see something positive; better days are coming."

Proverbs 23:12 "Apply your heart to instruction, and your ears to words of knowledge."

Romans 12:2 instructs us, *"Do not conform any longer to the pattern of this world but be transformed by the renewing of your mind. Then you can test and approve God's will—His good, pleasing, and perfect will"*. Amidst the evil and corruption prevalent in the world, you must transform through the renewal of your mind. This transformation is not a one-time event but a gradual and continuous process. Altering your habits, patterns, and focus can fundamentally change your life. Transformation involves changing the external appearance and one's character or condition. It means converting to a new way of thinking and being. Renewal means to make something new again, to restore it to its original state of freshness or perfection. Renewing your mind revolutionizes your thought processes, paving the way for a more fulfilling life. A mind reprogrammed to think like Christ enables us to discern and embrace the truth fully. When we are transformed and renew our minds, we align our thoughts with God's rather than succumbing to the world's dictates. The world incessantly tempts us to lead a life marked by sin and selfishness, to follow the crowd for the sake of visibility and acceptance. Once transformed and our minds renewed, we can anticipate nothing but greatness. Why? Because we have become overcomes.

Our minds have undergone spiritual regeneration, and our bodies have been revitalized, enabling us to make comprehensive changes and rebuild. You can confidently bid farewell to insecurity and warmly welcome a newfound magnificence. What lies before us now is sheer greatness. Greatness is not merely an achievement or a reward; it emerges from within when our lives are harmonious, and we view change as a chance for enhancement. It is crucial to become more self-aware of our actions.

Setting personal goals and documenting them allows for daily reflection and motivation. It is important to identify a role model—someone respected and trustworthy. Above all, learning to love oneself is fundamental. Greatness necessitates preparation, aligning our actions with our aspirations. Consider where you choose to plant yourself, opting to serve others rather than focusing solely on yourself. Growth signifies evolving into the leader or individual you are destined to be. It is common to be derailed by past traumas, failed relationships, or illnesses, losing sight of our focus. However, upon reflecting on our lives, we can acknowledge our blessings and express gratitude to God for His grace and mercy. You have endured trials, rain, and storms, yet you have prevailed because of God's grace and mercy. God loves you deeply and has an extraordinary plan for your life.

John 3:16 affirms, *"For God so loved the world that He gave His only begotten Son, that whoever believes in Him should not perish but have everlasting life"*. Jesus highlighted that thieves intend to steal, kill, and destroy. However, Jesus came so we could have life more abundantly, to live it to the fullest until it overflows. An overcomer is someone who successfully navigates through difficulties. Despite facing potentially frustrating situations, an overcomer chooses to press on through any conflict or struggle. You did not give up, cave in, or throw in the towel. Instead, you held firm. Remember, it is not about the depth of the fall but the height of your rebound. Though the future may be uncertain, be assured that letting go means falling into the hands of God, who is always in control.

On a Saturday afternoon, my friend Linda came over to visit my mother and me. True to form, she immediately asked, "What do you have to eat?" Heading into the den to catch up with my mother, I went to the kitchen to prepare something for us to eat. Once ready, the three of us sat down to enjoy the meal together. Filled with joy, Linda kept us laughing with her comments about the meal I had prepared. After finishing our meal, I cleared everything away. Linda then shared about her surgery in 2016, a six-hour procedure on her neck. Following the surgery, she was transferred to a rehabilitation center for three weeks, where she received restorative and therapeutic care to better her condition and physical function.

One day, while Linda was in the exercise room, she passed out for about five minutes. This incident was a result of the type of surgery she had undergone, which impeded proper blood flow to her head. Eight to nine months later, Linda began to experience excruciating pain and complications. An MRI revealed that she had a herniated disc at the top of her spine, leading to paralysis on her right side for three weeks. Despite this daunting challenge, Linda's Faith did not waver. She clung to hope and belief, confident that God would heal her body. She felt she had much more to accomplish and could not do so if she remained paralyzed. As the weeks passed, Linda's Faith only grew stronger. One day, she discovered she could move her fingers; another day, she moved her hand and, eventually, her arm. Filled with joy and tears streaming down her face, Linda knew the Lord had answered her prayers. Linda often reflected on this scripture from Matthew 21:22: *"And all things, whatever you shall ask in prayer, believing, you shall receive."*

As we begin to align with our true identity, God starts affirming it. Ephesians 5:1,2 guides us, *"Be ye therefore followers of God, as dear children; And walk in love, as Christ also hath loved us."* Embracing our identity as beloved children of God, co-heirs with Christ, changes everything. With this understanding, greatness awaits, and as we grasp our identity in Christ, we stand in a position of strength. Who am I? I am not defined by others' opinions; I am defined by what God says about me.

I am covered, I am so loved, I am more than a conqueror, I am a child of God, I am known, I am brave, I can do all things through Christ who strengthens me. You, too, as an overcomer, have emerged from darkness, and no matter life's challenges, remember, you are destined to overcome. Stay inspired, pursue greatness, and embrace nothing short of success. True greatness arises from surmounting challenges, not avoiding them altogether. While this does not imply recklessness, it encourages attentiveness to God's guidance. Although the heart's contents remain hidden, God alone discerns its depths.

**"I am an overcomer, praise God!
Goodbye, Insecurities, and Hello Gorgeous!!!"**

Chapter Review

1. **Continuous Transformation through Mind Renewal:** Emphasizing Romans 12:2, this chapter highlights the importance of not conforming to the world's patterns but being transformed by renewing the mind. This transformation is not a one-off event but a lifelong process that involves changing habits, thoughts, and actions to align with a higher purpose and moral standards.

2. **The Power of Faith and Hope:** Through personal anecdotes and biblical references, this chapter underscores the significance of Faith and hope in overcoming adversity. Linda's story is a testament to the belief that Faith in God can bring miraculous healing and strength to overcome severe challenges.

3. **Embracing Greatness as a Journey:** This chapter establishes that Greatness is not an external achievement but an internal state of being that reflects harmony, self-awareness, and the

willingness to embrace change positively. It is about aligning actions with aspirations and becoming the individual or leader one is destined to be.

4. **The Importance of Self-Love and Gratitude**: Learning to love oneself and acknowledging one's blessings are central to this transformation journey. Expressing gratitude, setting personal goals, and having role models are practical steps toward embracing one's Greatness.

5. **Overcoming Challenges with Resilience:** The chapter delineates that being an overcomer means navigating through difficulties with resilience, not giving up in the face of obstacles, and learning from every experience. It emphasizes the importance of rebounding from setbacks and continuously striving for personal growth and improvement.

6. **Faith as the Foundation for Overcoming:** Through references to scriptures and personal testimony, it is clear that Faith plays a crucial role

in overcoming life's challenges. Believing in something greater than oneself and trusting in God's plan and timing are depicted as essential to achieving greatness and overcoming adversities.

7. **Community and Sharing:** The shared meal and conversations between the narrator, Linda, and the narrator's mother illustrate the importance of community, support, and sharing life's journey. These interactions highlight the value of encouragement and the strength found in relationships.

Chapter Five

POEM

With Faith as our shield and victory in sight,
We march forth into the night.
Belief fuels our journey, a relentless drive,
In the power of Faith, we come alive.

Challenges loom, large and fierce,
Yet Faith whispers, "You can pierce."
Each step forward is a testament to true,
To the victories we're destined to accrue.

Let Faith be the wind beneath your wings,
As you soar above mundane things.
For in the heart where Faith resides,
A well of endless victory abides.

FAITH AND VICTORY

"To be prepared is half the victory."

"Where there is unity, there is always victory."

"Accept the challenges so that you can feel the exhilaration of victory."

"If you dare to begin, you dare to succeed."

"If you believe in yourself, are dedicated and proud, and never quit, you'll be a winner."

When seeking intervention or a miracle in your life, it's essential to approach with Faith, holding firm in the belief that God's promises will manifest. He is an unfailing deity whose promises are steadfast; His words are imbued with truth and never fail to achieve their intended purpose. Referencing Isaiah 55:11: *"So shall my word be that goes forth from my mouth; It shall not return to me void, but it shall accomplish what I please, And it shall prosper in the thing for which I sent it."*

Isaiah 55:11 elucidates a profound truth: when the Lord dispatches His word, it operates akin to a seed planted within the human heart, destined to flourish and bear fruit. This metaphor underscores the transformative power of God's word, highlighting its ability to effect change and foster growth within us. While the full extent of God's plans often eludes our comprehension, their magnitude surpassing our understanding, we are reassured that His word is purposeful. It is designed to fulfil His specific intentions for us, each directive meticulously orchestrated to guide, enrich, and transform our lives.

The challenges and circumstances we encounter are not arbitrary; they are purposefully allowed by God. Far from intending our downfall, these experiences are tailored to sculpt us into the individuals He envisions us to become. Through trials, we are shaped, refined, and primed for the roles He has in store for us, demonstrating His unwavering commitment to our growth and His masterful design for our lives. At times, we find ourselves trapped by our doubts and insecurities, becoming entangled in a web of anxiety, fear, and self-doubt. To navigate through these tumultuous emotions, it is essential to cultivate a profound sense of Faith.

Referencing Matthew 21:22: *"And whatever you ask in prayer, you will receive if you have faith.* "This scripture emphasizes the transformative power of Faith, illuminating the path for those who choose to believe while casting shadows on the paths of those who do not. Faith acts as a beacon, guiding us through the darkest times and offering hope when all seems lost. It is the foundation upon which a fractured world can find its way back to light, providing the resilience needed to persevere through life's trials. Faith assures us of God's presence by our side, empowering us to understand that He is nurturing our growth with every challenge we face.

Embrace the belief that each difficult situation harbors the potential for something positive to emerge. Unbeknownst to many, Faith plays a role in our everyday actions, guiding us in seemingly mundane tasks with trust and confidence. For instance, when we sit in a chair, we do so with the implicit Faith that it will support us without giving it a second thought. Similarly, God desires for us to place our trust in Him with the same simplicity and assurance.

The biblical account of Noah serves as a profound example of unwavering Faith. Informed by God about the impending flood, a catastrophe unseen and unfathomable at the time, Noah embraced his Faith amidst fear. He undertook the monumental task of building an ark, a feat driven by his steadfast belief in God's word. Through his actions, Noah secured his family's survival and underscored the immeasurable strength that comes from placing one's Faith in the Divine.

Through Faith, Sarah, who was barren, found the strength to conceive and deliver a child well beyond her childbearing years. By Faith, Moses' parents concealed him for three months after his birth. They recognized his extraordinary destiny and were fearless in the face of the king's decree. Through Faith, the walls of Jericho collapsed after the Israelites circled them for seven days, leading them to a triumphant victory. A friend shared her story of Faith and triumph with me. In 2011, she found herself deeply thankful to Jesus, the cornerstone of her life. Without the Lord's guidance and her family's unwavering support, navigating the challenges she faced would have been significantly harder. She occasionally felt discomfort in her breast.

During a routine self-examination one day, she discovered a lump. Concerned, she consulted a doctor and underwent a mammogram. After the scans, the doctor invited her into his office to discuss the findings.

He revealed the presence of a lump and recommended surgery. Her heart raced as she processed the news. The doctor admitted he had never encountered a case quite like hers before and expressed his desire to consult with a colleague about her situation.

When it was time for my surgery, I was in the care of two surgeons. My primary doctor was responsible for removing the affected tissue from my breast, while a plastic surgeon was tasked with the reconstruction. The plastic surgeon explained that he would insert a device about the size of a quarter into my breast, along with saline implants, to aid in the reconstruction process. Thankfully, the surgery went well. Afterwards, I had to follow up with the doctor annually for ten years to undergo blood work and maintain the procedure's success. From 2011 to 2021, I have been cancer-free, and I attribute this blessing to my God, Lord, and Savior. It was God's doing; He worked through the hands of the surgeons. I am an overcomer. I maintained my Faith throughout and have now achieved victory. Amen!

Romans 10:17 says, *"Faith comes by hearing, and hearing by the word of God."* Victory is for those who persevere the most. The greatest victory one can achieve is conquering oneself; to be defeated by oneself is the most shameful and vile outcome. Remember, your victory is just around the corner. NEVER GIVE UP! Success is like climbing a staircase, step by step, rather than simply walking through a door. The small victories we collect on our long journey fuel our confidence, keep our joy alive, and push us to stay motivated. Remember, criticism is just noise on the sidelines; keep your eyes on the path ahead.

1 Corinthians 15:57 gives us a powerful message: "But thanks be to God, who gives us the victory through our Lord Jesus Christ." This verse is a beautiful reminder that our triumphs, big and small, are not solely of our own making. They are gifts from God, achieved through our Faith in Jesus Christ. It tells us that the true victory—over challenges, doubts, and even death—comes through the grace and love of God. Psalm 28:7 offers another layer of encouragement: "The Lord is my strength and my shield; my heart

trusts in Him." This is a personal declaration of Faith, where the Psalmist sees God as their source of strength and protection. It is a call to remember where our true support and power come from, especially when we are facing uphill battles. Trusting in God gives us an unshakeable foundation, no matter what we encounter on our journey to success.

What do faith and victory mean?

Faith is victory because it signifies God's triumph over us and within us. It is proof that God has established a permanent presence within us, forging an eternal bond through Christ. In 1 John 5:4, tells us, *"For whatsoever is born of God overcometh the world: and this is the victory that overcometh the world, even our faith."* Here, "faith" is identified as our victory. Every believer is an overcomer, victorious by possessing eternal life in Christ and experiencing abundant life now.

Belief in our potential for success empowers us to influence our thoughts, emotions, and actions. This mindset cultivates focus, positivity, and resilience, leading to a self-fulfilling prophecy where our beliefs shape our outcomes.

Ways to demonstrate faith:

1. Listen with an open mind: Intelligent individuals are always open to learning.
2. Avoid negativity.
3. Pray about it.
4. Be a peacemaker.
5. Keep your word.

During challenging times, spend moments in prayer, acknowledging God's greatness. Connect with fellow believers and focus on things greater than your circumstances. Serving others can help you perceive God's presence amidst difficulties, fostering trust that He will intervene. While God loves us, our sinful nature necessitates experiencing failure, pain, and struggle. Through these trials, we grow stronger in faith, drawing closer to Him and moving away from sin.

By nurturing faith, we shape a mindset that is focused, positive, and resilient. This mindset, in turn, guides our actions and shapes our outcomes, leading to success.

James 1:2-4 *"Consider it pure joy, my brothers and sisters, whenever you face trials of many kinds, because you know that the testing of your faith produces perseverance. Let perseverance finish its work so that you may be mature and complete, not lacking anything."* Fear may try to overwhelm you, but remember, God is all-powerful and provides the strength you need. Isaiah 41:10 reassures us: *"So do not fear, for I am with you; do not be dismayed, for I am your God. I will strengthen you and help you; I will uphold you with my righteous right hand."*

Our faith is the key to victory. The path to overcoming the world lies in faith in Jesus Christ, the Son of God. Philippians 4:6,7 reminds us: *"Be careful for nothing, but in everything by prayer and supplication with thanksgiving let your request be made known unto God. And the peace of God, which passeth all understanding, shall keep your hearts and minds through Christ Jesus."*

With faith, victory is yours!

Goodbye Insecurities and Hello Gorgeous

Chapter Review

1. **Faith as a Foundation for Miracles:** The essential message is that Faith is not just a feeling but a foundational principle for witnessing miracles and divine interventions in life. Believing in God's promises and steadfastness is crucial for experiencing the manifestation of His word.

2. **The Power of God's Word:** Isaiah 55:11 emphasizes the potency and purposefulness of God's word. It is likened to a seed that is destined to bear fruit once planted in the human heart. This illustrates the transformative and growth-inducing effect of divine communication.

3. **Purposeful Challenges for Growth:** Life's challenges are not random but are allowed by God with a purpose. They are meant to mold and refine us into God's vision for our lives, demonstrating that trials are not punitive but developmental.

4. **The Role of Faith in Overcoming Doubt and Fear:** Faith is presented as the antidote to doubt, fear, and insecurity. It is a beacon that lights up dark times, providing hope and strength to persevere through trials and challenges.

5. **Victory through Faith and Perseverance:** The narrative reinforces that victory—over personal battles like health issues or spiritual ones—is achieved through Faith and perseverance. It's underscored that triumphs are not solely the result of human effort but are gifts from God, facilitated by our belief and trust in His power and plan.

Epilogue

As we draw the curtain on this journey, remember the resilient spirit encapsulated in the words: "Throw me to the wolves, and I will return leading the pack!" This is not just a statement; it is a testament to the power of faith and the courage to defy the odds. You have seen that what seemed impossible is merely a steppingstone to achieving your true potential.

You have transitioned from dreams to reality, embracing the essence of your true self over the shadows of who you thought you were supposed to be. This transformation mirrors the wisdom found in Proverbs 3:5-6, which urges us to "Trust in the Lord with all your heart and lean not on your own understanding; in all your ways submit to Him, and He will make your paths straight." It is a call to wholeheartedly embrace faith, letting it guide you to clarity and purpose beyond human comprehension.

Consider the metaphor of the empty wagon, noisy and attention-seeking, against the filled wagon, steady and purposeful. This symbolizes our journey with God—a path where the clamor of insecurities and doubts fades away as we fill our hearts with His presence and purpose.

As you close this book, let it not be an end but a commencement of your beautiful, fearless journey ahead. Embrace God's presence fully, and let it lead you to the new beginnings waiting just beyond the horizon of your faith. Goodbye, Insecurities and Hello Gorgeous Journey with God.